HCB-ANGUS

A PICTORIAL RECORD

AIDAN FISHER

AMBERLEY

First published 2013

Amberley Publishing
The Hill, Stroud
Gloucestershire, GL5 4EP

www.amberley-books.com

British Library Cataloguing in Publication Data.
A catalogue record for this book is available from the British
Library.

ISBN 978-1-4456-1682-7
E-Book ISBN 978-1-4456-1697-1

Typeset in 10pt on 12pt Sabon.
Typesetting and Origination by Amberley Publishing.
Printed in the UK.

Introduction

This volume does not purport to tell the story of HCB (Engineering), later HCB-Angus, but to be a chronological presentation of typical vehicles produced over the lifetime of the company. Similarly, the commercial vehicle body-building arm of the company is not covered as this is unrecorded in any meaningful way other than the few photographs that remain.

The company produced some 6,500 fire appliances over some fifty years of activity (if we discount the couple produced as 'one-offs' during the mid-1930s); many were identical, as in an order for a group of vehicles, but HCB-Angus prided themselves in producing just what the customer wanted so there were many variations on a theme.

What is presented in this volume is a representative sample, as far as is possible, and the photographs are presented in chronological order. HCB-Angus placed a builder's plate on every vehicle (except for when the customer specifically prohibited any builder's information to be displayed) and on this plate was stamped the vehicle's unique body serial number, by which the appliances in this book are referred to.

HCB (Engineering) gave each individual vehicle a number against an order so, for instance, an order for four vehicles may attract the body serial numbers 1246, 1247, 1248 and 1249. However, during the 1960s, after the involvement of Angus Fire when the company became HCB-Angus, a new system was introduced where all the vehicles had the same basic serial number with a slash followed by the individual indicator. Therefore, an order for four vehicles would now be 5643/1, 5643/2, 5643/3, and 5436/4

The vast majority of the photographs in this book come from the photographic archive left by HCB-Angus on their closure but some have come from sources known and unknown. I have to thank Ken Reid, Simon Rowley, Gary Chapman, Colin Carter and Ian Moore for their photographs and extend thanks to the unknown people whose photographs I have purchased 'in the field' and used within this volume and upon whose copyright I have unavoidably infringed. Credit will be given in future should such infringement be pointed out.

Finally, I must thank Amberley Publishing for producing this work and Louis Archard, in particular, for looking after its production.

Aidan Fisher

These Surrey Dodges were the first fire appliances built by HCB (Engineering). OW 2987 was built as an airport appliance for the fledgling Southampton Airport. OW 4021 on the other hand was constructed as a domestic appliance for the local authority. Both were a subcontract from a local garage who had tendered against a specification from a local Dodge agent. There were to be no more fire appliances produced before the Second World War. (*Alan House*)

Where to start?

HCB (Engineering) was set up in the immediate post-war era on the foundations of a pre-war coach-building company (and had produced two fire appliances in the mid-1930s). They were working on contracts producing new cabs for AEC, Thornycroft and the Great Western Railway Company as well as doing refurbishment work of all types including work on NFS fire appliances, these being well worn from their wartime work. The company acquired a Commer chassis scuttle and produced a water tender appliance, and – to their surprise – this sold before completion to Royal Berkshire Fire Brigade. A second chassis was purchased and this was constructed as a pump escape, again being sold to the same brigade before completion. This experience suggested to the company that this was the way forward and serious consideration was given as to how they could go forward in a profitable manner.

After the Second World War, the Central Fire Brigades Advisory Council's Joint Committee on Design and Development of Appliances and Equipment issued specifications for different types of fire appliance, the JCDD specifications, and the company used these as a starting point. There was a need to carry a crew (usually driver, officer and four crew) together with all the water, pumps and kit specified for the particular vehicle – though this was flexible. A medium-weight chassis was needed, petrol engined (as the diesels of the day were very slow-revving and heavy) and preferably forward-control configuration to keep the vehicle as compact as possible. It is not by accident that the company had chosen a Commer chassis for their first ventures – it was forward control and was fitted with a petrol engine that had the advantage of being slant fitted to lessen cab intrusion. But there were few others to pick from and the company had to produce vehicles that were bonneted – the Leyland Comet and the Commer Kew featured in early production for instance.

Bedford came into the picture very strongly in the early 1950s with the production, firstly, of the SB coach chassis (late 1951) and then the SH special fire engine chassis in 1954. The RL introduced in 1953 gave a 4x4 capability to the long version of the S chassis. All these were capable forward-control chassis whose only downside was the very high step up to the driver/officers doors as they were directly above the front wheel. All these chassis had a 10-ton rating so were capable of the heaviest fire engine duties of the day.

Bedford also introduced the A (1953), C and D (1957) and J (1958) series of bonneted vehicles, available in 1–7-ton versions, which HCB adopted as the basis for many appliances having first worked with Vauxhall Motors in the provision of a forward-control version. A similar conversion was organised for the bonneted Dodge. This body style was also available on the Commer chassis but in far fewer numbers.

Thus, HCB (Engineering) design department had secured for themselves a solid base upon which to produce the majority of appliances through this first decade of production.

An ex-wartime Dodge from the NFS, this appliance – GXM 40, together with a number of others, was renovated by HCB (Engineering) for service with the Isle of Wight Fire Brigade. It was constructed as a Water Tender A type (WrT A), that is had an on-board water tank that was plumbed into a light portable pump (LPP) that had been separately mounted onto the chassis. As can be seen from the control gear behind the officer's door these appliances also had an engine-driven hose reel pump. (*HCB-Angus*)

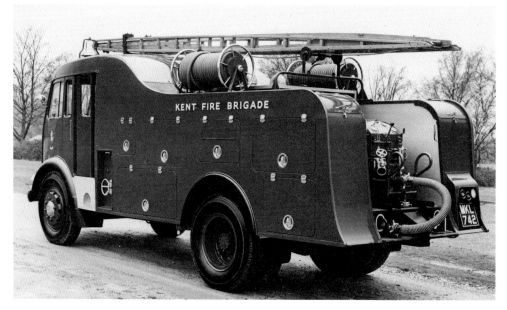

MKL 742, also a WrT A, was one of a pair built in 1950 for Kent Fire Brigade on a Commer 21A chassis. Again, a separate hose reel pump was fitted. HCB (Engineering) went on to build over twenty similar appliances during the period 1951–52 together with a number of what were described as Pump Salvage Tenders (PST). *(HCB-Angus)*

Worcester City & County Fire Brigade preferred a Leyland product and specified a Comet chassis for the construction of four appliances in 1951. While normal control did keep engine noise out of the cab, it did mean that the crew cab was somewhat restricted in space as attempts were made to keep overall length down. These vehicles were a full pumping appliance, having an engine-driven pump and a 300-gallon water tank. This appliance was registered FFK 350, s45, and entered service in 1952. (*HCB-Angus*)

Fife Fire Brigade purchased four WrT As in 1952 based on the Commer 45A chassis. This one, s84 registered LFG 176, unusually for the year, carries an aluminium ladder. (*Ken Reid*)

JDL 540 and 541 were Commer 21A chassis built up by HCB as Dual Purpose (DP) machines for the Isle of Wight Fire Brigade, entering service in 1952. They carried a 55-foot Merryweather escape as well as having an engine driven pump and a 100-gallon water tank. Notice the pump controls again on the side of the vehicle but note it is to enable pump control when the escape is still mounted. (*HCB-Angus*)

7

The arrival of the Big Bedford, as it was known, opened up new avenues for appliance builders. Croydon Fire Brigade ordered this Emergency Tender (ET) from HCB late in 1952. Later in life it was modified and saw service as a Control Unit. (*HCB-Angus*)

Worcester City & County Fire Brigade ordered a WrT from the company, s120 registered FFK 549, based on the Bedford coach chassis/scuttle. The SB scuttle is identifiable by the smoother front valance panel. (*HCB-Angus*)

Possibly the only disadvantage with the Big Bedford was the fact that entry to the cab by means of the manufacturer's doors was very high as it was immediately over the front wheels. HCB dealt with this by building from a chassis scuttle and not providing 'front' doors – all the crew had to enter by way of the jackknife rear doors! Doncaster Fire Brigade ordered this appliance, s107, registered LDT 510, early in 1953. It complied with the new JDDC specification for WrT B – carrying 400 gallons of water and having a vehicle engine-driven pump capable of 500 gallons per minute (gpm) at 100 pounds per square inch (psi) and carrying a 35-foot ladder. In this case, as in many others during the 1950s and even into the 1960s, the Dennis No. 2 pump was salvage, having been taken from a wartime trailer pump. (*HCB-Angus*)

Rochdale Fire Brigade ordered an Emergency Tender (ET) from HCB in early 1954. Delivered on s160 and registered MDK 234 the basis was a cut-and-shut Bedford SB chassis. Shown here in service sporting the white front that typified appliances from this brigade, it is clearly carrying a lot of kit judging from the lean to the rear. (*HCB-Angus*)

The Bedford SH was to form the basis for many hundreds of HCB appliances supplied to many brigades. The flowing roofline gave the appliance a pleasing appearance. An early modification was the change from the short doors and external step to longer doors and an internal step, which improved the appearance further. This example was purchased by Southampton Fire Brigade on s163 as a full WrT B. (*HCB-Angus*)

This example, s199, registered NSF 200, was ordered by the South Eastern Fire Brigade as a pump (P) as it carried only 100 gallons of water. (*Ken Reid*)

Registered NBE 691, s202 was one of a pair of Bedford A3-chassised towing vehicles (TV) built for Lindsey County Fire Brigade in 1955 (though a further pair was ordered shortly after). The A3 was a bonneted vehicle and HCB made use of a semi-forward-control-scuttle assembly built by Neville's (Coachbuilders) of Southampton as an interim measure while they developed their own full-forward-control body. (*HCB-Angus*)

At this time Devon County Fire Service chose to stay with a bonneted vehicle and ordered four appliances built on the Dodge 123 chassis. One of the four, s208 registered UUO 305, is shown in HCB's yard demonstrating the mounting of the Light Portable Pump on a gantry over the main Dennis pump. (*HCB-Angus*)

Above left: Seen here is the prototype of the all-metal conversion that could be placed on both Bedford and Dodge chassis, in this case mounted on a Bedford J5. Though described as all metal, this, in fact, referred to the rear body construction, which was of steel angle and tube with aluminium panels – the cab front being a fibreglass moulding made in-house, quite a complex piece of moulding involving bespoke glass for the windscreen. (*HCB-Angus*)

Above right: Shown here is the rear of s274, one of the group of four ordered by Devon County Fire Service, on a Dodge chassis and registered XTA 302. The portable pump was carried on an ingenious cradle, fitted over the main pump and running on rollers in the rear bodywork between the lockers and the tank. The cradle could be slid out and remained supported at its inner ends while the LPP was removed. (*HCB-Angus*)

Below: XTA 302 seen here in service. A compact machine, they had no front doors and the crew doors were on runners and were slid to the rear to gain entry. This, plus the roller shutters on the lockers, meant they could operate in confined spaces without hindrance to crew or to locker access. (*Unknown*)

A plainer front moulding as seen on s288, registered 1508 HK, one of an order in 1957 for Essex County Fire Brigade for no less than fourteen identical appliances. The chassis of choice for this order was the Dodge 134 and the pump installation had four deliveries, a substantial number for a WrT. (*HCB-Angus*)

A unique appliance built for the Northern Area Fire Brigade is this Karrier-based appliance. While being tiny in size this appliance is a full blown WrT, just like its bigger brothers. This appliance still exists, though in a ruinous state. It was built on s460 and registered MST 400, being ordered in 1958. (*Andy Anderson*)

Brecon & Radnorshire Joint Fire Brigade purchased a pair of appliances built on the newly introduced Bedford J5 chassis in 1959. This one, s480, registered HEU 535, and its pair were provided with an HCB-designed semi-forward-control body. Why this was done rather than the established full-forward-control version is not clear. (*HCB-Angus*)

In 1958 Carlisle Fire Brigade ordered a single appliance built up on a Bedford C5 chassis. Note, it does not have quite the sweeping lines of the S type's body, being a little smaller. Registered PHH 101, the body carried s498. (*Andy Anderson*)

Lancashire County Fire Brigade embarked on a fleet-replacement program ordering no less than a dozen appliances on one order in 1958. This one, s511, registered 383 LDT, shows off the new forward-control conventional-construction body, where just the front panel is painted while the remainder of the body is stucco aluminium panelling. These appliances were unusual in having Hayward Tyler main pumps. (*HCB-Angus*)

Lanarkshire Fire Brigade ordered this single Bedford J5-chassised appliance, s526, registered VVD 111, as a comparison vehicle, as they also ordered a similarly specified Bedford S machine at the same time. Note that the brigade preferred the external step as it gave a larger floor surface within the appliance. (*HCB-Angus*)

In the late 1950s, the Ministry of Transport and Civil Aviation were seeking an ET to use on its airports and spent some time with HCB developing this group of vehicles being 4x4 Bedford RL-based. They had a considerable gestation time due to technical difficulties with the equipment they were to carry, but eventually twenty-two were to be delivered over some time. This example, s530, registered VXN 877, served most of its life at Penngran Moor followed by a brief period at Stansted Airport. (*HCB-Angus*)

S539, registered UDL 233, was a Dual Purpose (DP) appliance built for the Isle of Wight Fire Brigade. The appliance could carry a full complement of ladders, 45-foot escape, 35-foot extension and short extension, as here, but was then limited to 300 gallons of water or run as a WrT without the escape but carrying 400 gallons of water. (*Simon Rowley*)

A further example of the composite-structured Bedford J type, s575, registered 947 CNM, built for Bedfordshire Fire Service. Constructed in 1960, this appliance was one of the very first to carry a blue rotating beacon from new. Bedfordshire Fire Brigade, serving the M1, decided that they needed something conspicuous to identify their appliances when at work on the motorway – hence the beacon. (*HCB-Angus*)

Some brigades required the occasional 4x4 appliance and in this case Worcester City & County Fire Brigade ordered s588, registered 800 FFK, based on the Bedford RL chassis. The water capacity of the appliance was reduced to 300 gallons due to the increased weight of the basic vehicle. (*Unknown*)

Durham County Fire Brigade ordered a single Pump Escape (PE) s580, registered 204 JUP, in 1960 and it was constructed on a Bedford J4 with the all-metal form of construction. The escape is similarly an all-metal Merryweather version. Notice that this appliance, as all the others on this page, is now fitted with shutters rather than locker doors. These were of HCB's own construction, being pressed from sheet aluminium. (*HCB-Angus*)

The introduction by Bedford of the TK chassis in 1960 provided HCB with an even better base than the S type for a fire appliance. The company only utilised the scuttle A posts up as far as the bottom of the windscreen, preferring to build a cab from there up. In this way a wider and deeper view could be provided, despite having to use two flat screens rather than the original curved glass. LEN 999, s609, was one of the first, built for Bury Fire Brigade. Notice the high-specification chrome front bumper on this appliance. (*HCB-Angus*)

The Isle of Wight Fire Brigade was another early evaluator of the Bedford TK. This one, in all-paint finish, was in build at the same time as the Bury appliance, being s618, registered WDL 498. At this time, all Bedford TK fire appliances came with the 4.9-litre petrol engine, it being some years before a diesel that was fast-revving enough to be suitable was available. (*Simon Rowley*)

Shropshire Fire Brigade ordered s645, registration WUX 172, early in 1961 as a DP appliance built on a Commer 86A chassis. The Commer did not lend itself to front doors due to the front axle being well forward so the whole crew had to mount through the crew compartment, fitted in this instance with slam doors rather than HCB's favoured jackknife variety. (*HCB-Angus*)

Western Area Fire Brigade took delivery of several Hose Reel Tenders (HrT) based on the Austin/Morris FGK chassis, more usually seen as a 'trupenny bit' cabbed delivery van. This one, s704, registered THS 870, also still carries a pair of orange flashers on the cab, a practice becoming obsolete by this time. A 200-gallon tank was carried and a gearbox side-mounted pump fitted. (*HCB-Angus*)

In late 1961, Exeter City Fire Brigade ordered a DP appliance based on the Bedford TK, and s716, registered 444 EFJ, was the result. Although the pump is conventionally mounted at the rear the controls and deliveries were side mounted, rather awkwardly behind the access ladder rungs. (*HCB-Angus*)

Special Purposes appliances were frequently very much in the purview of the CFO so far as requirements went. This ET built for Suffolk and Ipswich Fire Service on s717, registered 928 LBJ, was one such. (*Unknown*)

West Sussex Fire Brigade ordered three WrTs in 1962 of the full-metal variety. Body serial 720, registered 43 EPO, is a survivor and is frequently seen on the rally field. (*HCB-Angus*)

This ET for Wigan Fire Brigade, s728, registration JEK 999, is of very similar construction to the one above, though their internal fitments were very different. However, one being all paint and the other stucco aluminium gives them a very different appearance. Note the translucent panels let into the roof edges for illumination of the interior. (*HCB-Angus*)

A new chassis for the company was the Land Rover. This formed the basis for a multitude of light firefighting vehicles during the life of the company. Shown is s769, a Series 2 supplied to Short Brothers of Belfast as a works fire engine and registered 5239 EZ. It carried 70 gallons of water that supplied a Coventry Climax pump, driven from the Land Rover's power take off. (*HCB-Angus*)

Built as an especially low-height appliance – note the front panel mounted bell and the ladder troughed into the roof line – s778 was built for the Somerset Fire Brigade on s778. Chassied on the Bedford J2 it had a reduced water capacity of 200 gallons. (*Unknown*)

Another new chassis at this time was the AEC 5GMLRH utilised here as the basis of a Pump Emergency Salvage Tender (PEST). It carried a great amount of kit – thus explaining the need for a heavier chassis. The AEC was not a popular chassis with HCB but was a regular in the works for those brigades requiring it as a basis for a vehicle. (*HCB-Angus*)

Another of the baby TJ-type appliances, 999 RHY was a HrT for Bristol City Fire Brigade built on s792. Notice the family resemblance but having no front doors, with all the crew having to use the crew doors. It carried 150 gallons of water, had a gearbox-mounted pump and a single hose reel mounted at the rear. It did, however, have a portable pump that can be seen here on its cradle. (*HCB-Angus*)

Yet another new chassis at this period of time was the Thornycroft Nubian – a real heavyweight. This crash tender was built on s800 for the Bristol Aircraft Fire Brigade and served at Filton Airfield. It was to be the first of many Nubians to pass through the works. (*HCB-Angus*)

Devon County Fire Service ordered s817, registered 993 NUO, as a single DP appliance on the Bedford TJ6 chassis and bodied with the all-metal style of body. The Merryweather escape was quite a bulky bit of kit when slung on the back of these compact machines! It carried 300 gallons of water and had a Coventry Climax pump. (*HCB-Angus*)

A Thames Trader was an odd choice of chassis – in fact this was the only one to pass through the company's hands – but it was the choice of Oxford City Fire Brigade for the construction of this ET. Registered 288 RFC, it carried body s826. (*HCB-Angus*)

A number of appliances were built using the Austin/Morris FGK range of mid-weight vehicles and this one, s872, registered LSB 148, was one of only three that were constructed as full-pumping appliances utilising a Prestage remotely mounted PTO as the pump drive. This appliance survives in the care of the the Fire Service National Museum. (*HCB-Angus*)

In 1964 the Ministry of Transport and Civil Aviation ordered nine of these Water/Foam Tenders (WrFoT), followed by four more over the next couple of years. Based on the Bedford RL 4x4 chassis they had very basic bodywork containing a 500-gallon water tank, a 75-gallon foam compound tank with a Coventry Climax pump engine driven. This example, registered 19 GXE, s901 served at Sumburgh and later at Uist. (*HCB-Angus*)

Bristol City Fire Brigade obtained this standard Bedford TK-based Foam Carrier (FoC) s909, registered 999 VHY, from HCB as transport for 500 gallons of foam compound together with ancillary equipment. The stowage arrangement for 100 5-gallon drums was the subject of some discussion between the company and the chief fire officer as he wished them to be accessible from the outside of the vehicle, which caused some racking problems. (*HCB-Angus*)

The East Pakistan authorities ordered eight capable WrT tender appliances on one order, this being s989. Not being bound by the JCDD specifications, many variations on the theme of 'fire engine' were specified by customers abroad. This appliance has a 1000-gallon tank to supply its pump as well as carrying the usual firefighting gear. (*HCB-Angus*)

The Libyan regime was a big customer of HCB before the political situation became difficult. This Land Rover, s1037, is one of three Rescue Tenders (RT) on the long wheelbase chassis. They had a firefighting capability as well as carrying a larger than usual quantity of rescue equipment. (*HCB-Angus*)

Lindsey County Fire
Brigade ordered this
ET on a Bedford SB
coach chassis (in
order to obtain a
lower floor level) in
late 1964. Registered
BBE 157B, S1041, it
unusually retained
its Bedford scuttle
rather than be
fitted with the HCB
fibreglass version.
(*HCB-Angus*)

AIA 7348 was a
standard Land
Rover S2 S1046
appliance for
Duncan Logan Ltd.
Unusually for a UK
order, it carried a
Francis rolling siren
with the red centre
light. (*Unknown*)

Perak, a Malaysian
state, purchased the
only Unimog, S1048,
to pass through the
company's hands.
Built up as an
ET, it has the the
Unimog's legendary
off-road capability
and is carrying
an alloy ladder
by Merryweather,
timber not having a
long life in tropical
counties. (*HCB-
Angus*)

The Malawian authorities commissioned the building of a pair of crash tenders for their state airports based on the Bedford RL but fitted with normal wheels with pairs at the rear. Built with a roof-mounted monitor with an operator's plinth behind the cab, they carried 700 gallons of water, 170 of foam compound and had a 220-lb dry-powder installation. This works photo shows one of the pair s1055. (*HCB-Angus*)

The use of the Leyland Comet (fitted with the LAD cab) was an unusual choice, as was the typically American styling, but this is what the customer wanted. Constructed for the Chilean oil industry, this FoT, carrying body s1063, was one of a pair supplied in 1965 by HCB-Angus, as they were now known, to that country. The appliance carried 100 gallons of water and 1,000 gallons of foam compound. One of these appliances had a bad start when the operator burst the pump on the very first day in operation, running it flat out against closed deliveries, forgetting that the hydrant supply was already at very high pressure. (*HCB-Angus*)

HCB-Angus had entered into an agreement with Simon Engineering whereby customers wishing to purchase a Hydraulic Platform (HP) or a Pump Hydraulic Platform (PHP) would do so from Simon Engineering, who would fit the turret and booms, and then HCB-Angus would build the remainder of the body before delivery to the customer. s1070 was a PHP fitted with 65-foot booms, built on a Bedford TK supplied to the South African authorities; many more were to follow. (*HCB-Angus*)

Leeds City Fire Brigade ordered s1074, registered DNW 639C, in 1965 as a Foam Carrier (FC). Built on the standard Bedford TK chassis/cab it was equipped to carry 200 gallons of foam compound in 5-gallon tins. (*HCB-Angus*)

While not firefighting vehicles, riot-control trucks have the same characteristics – water, pump and delivery! HCB-Angus built a pair in 1965 on Bedford chassis for the Libyan Government, this one being s1112. They carried 1,100 gallons of water and could douse themselves with water while moving (as defence against fire), as well as delivering to the remotely controlled monitor jet. (*HCB-Angus*)

Middlesbrough Airport purchased this Thornycroft Nubian, s1128, registered DXG 969D, to comply with civil aviation requirements for airport protection. It carried 800 gallons of water, 100 gallons of foam compound and a 150-lb dry-powder installation. Unusually, all the controls for the firefighting equipment were placed at the rear of the appliance as a design requirement but it was not too successful an arrangement. (*HCB-Angus*)

Durban Fire Department, South Africa, ordered a single appliance on s1135. It looks like a standard WrT but, in fact, only carries 150 gallons of water. It was also fitted with HCB-Angus's own water pump. (*HCB-Angus*)

The TJ series Bedfords continued in production despite the success of the Bedford TK as a fire vehicle chassis. Durham County Fire Brigade purchased s1140, NUP 598D, as one of an order for a pair of Pump Escapes (PE). These appliances were fitted with HCB-Angus's own design of fire pump. (*HCB-Angus*)

East Pakistan ordered a pair of lightweight appliances, this being s1246, based on the normal-control Bedford TJ1. They were HRTs, having but 100 gallons of water on board and a gearbox-mounted water pump. The crew travelled in the shelter constructed on the pick-up's bed. They were successful, as many more were ordered later. (*HCB-Angus*)

In 1965, Kent Fire Brigade prepared a detailed specification for a new WrT, including the suggestions of the firefighters themselves. The end result was built on the Commer VSAKS 741 chassis and the brigade ordered twelve appliances in their first order in 1965. They carried 425 gallons of water and the Merryweather 45-foot extending ladder, alloy ladders beginning to replace timber at this time. This example s1270, registered EKM 102C, is seen on the tilt table undergoing a stability test, a requirement for all new designs of fire engine. (*HCB-Angus*)

The Middle Years

The 1950s were busy times for British manufacturing, still recovering from the war with the need to develop new products, yet being stifled by the lack of materials and the need to 'export or die'. Earlier mention was made of the design work that the company had undertaken and the commitment to Bedford products that had been made. Dodge and Commer were similarly supported but to a lesser extent.

By the 1960s, things were to change. The Bedford TK had been announced and that rapidly took the place, in even higher numbers, of the S type as a chassis of choice. Land Rover had eventually agreed to approve the conversion of its vehicles to fire appliances thus opening a new route to lighter appliances. The middle of the decade saw the Ford Transit appearing to transform that market – and provide the company with yet another avenue to follow.

During the decade, however, the Ford Motor Company announced the D series of chassis; these also became favourites with some brigades, and Commer had uprated to the VAKS chassis, maintaining their place. Heavier chassis were needed and a smattering of AEC and ERF products began to appear on client specifications. Thornycroft had already taken their place as the basis for major crash tender chassis provision.

Late in the 1960s, the Commer name was to disappear and be replaced by Dodge, the first of the K850s to be delivered in 1970. These were very competitive with the Ford D series as they were of similar weight and also offered the advantage (over Bedford) of having a tilt cab.

Production marched on, with ever-larger numbers of these chassis passing though the works with just the odd alternative offering a change. At one point the company was turning out one complete vehicle per day, a considerable achievement considering the choices to be had.

Seen here on station is s1273, registered FKM 112D, from the first batch of the Kent Fire Brigade Commer VAKS 741 WrT. Features shown (among the many suggestions of the firefighters) are the vision panel in the officers' door and the extended front bumper and grab rail to give a man stand at the front of the appliance. (*Roger Mardon*)

As Simon Engineering developed ever-longer versions of their Snorkel, bigger and heavier chassis were required. City of Lincoln Fire Brigade was to receive the first HP constructed by HCB-Angus on the ERF 8484 SR chassis. This had a full crew cab; later HPs were to have just a driver and officer on board. The Simon platform was an 85-foot version, the vehicle was registered EFE 597E and HCB-Angus body s1306. The ERF chassis was to be developed into a full-blown fire-appliance chassis/cab with HCB-Angus working with ERF/Jennings in the development of the double cab. (*HCB-Angus*)

The ubiquitous Bedford RL was again the basis of a pair of appliances for the Libyan oil industry. Shown is s1307 fitted as a FoT with an elliptical tank containing 500 gallons of foam compound. These appliances relied on the refinery hydrant system to provide the water for the foam making capability. (*HCB-Angus*)

Nottingham City Fire Brigade ordered a unique appliance in 1968 described as a Water Crash Tender (WrCT). Based on an AEC TGM4R, s1334, registered LTV 999F, it had an advanced specification including a full water-pumping capacity, a front-mounted winch that could also be used as a lifting arrangement with the retracting beam at the rear and an air compressor system, also engine driven. (*HCB-Angus*)

The area around the Huntingdon & Peterborough Fire Brigade's working area was mostly rural so it was decided that a pair of 4x4 appliances was required. The firefighting specification is straightforward WrT but the drive train is 4x4, provided by the Bedford RL, this time standing on off-road single tyres. HEW 148E is one of the pair on HCB-Angus body s1367. (*HCB-Angus*)

When the Ford Motor Company developed the D600 series, they offered a fire chassis and HCB-Angus took it up for development. Illustrated is one such, the 'Lo Cost' option, where there is no alteration to the manufacture's tilt cab (something new) and the crew section and body are completely separate. Gloucestershire Fire Brigade took a number of these appliances and s1429 is shown here, registered KDF 454F, one of the initial pair. (*HCB-Angus*)

The Ford Transit, when it was introduced, took the medium-van sector by storm and it was to form the basis for many light two-wheel-drive pumping appliances (L2P). The works demonstrator, s1445, is shown here as it did the rounds of potential customers. HCB-Angus developed their own drive line PTO so that the road engine could be utilised to drive the main Coventry Climax pump which drew from a 60-gallon water tank. This vehicle eventually entered service registered GBE 265E and in the ownership of Courtaulds Engineering. (*HCB-Angus*)

The ERF 84PS chassis became used in a limited way in the production of what the author considers some of the most handsome appliances. London Fire Brigade ordered three PE appliances, this one being s1577, registered SMH 347. They were equipped with London's own pattern 50-foot escape, carried 300 gallons of water and utilised a Coventry Climax pump. (*HCB-Angus*)

Nottinghamshire ordered a pair of PE on the ERF 84 PF chassis for delivery in 1969. Seen here is s1633, which eventually carried the registration SAL 998F, equipped with a Merryweather Escape, 400 gallons of water and a 500 gpm pump. Its sister appliance is preserved and is located at the Hall of Flame Museum, Phoenix,USA. (*HCB-Angus*)

Warrington Fire Brigade purchased but one appliance from HCB-Angus, an ET on s1672, registered NED 101G. It was no ordinary Bedford TK ET as it carried experimental High Expansion Foam equipment, thought at the time to be an advantageous method of smothering fires. It was not a great success and the vehicle worked more in a conventional ET role. (*HCB-Angus*)

Seen here is s1673, an AEC TGM4R for Blackpool Fire Brigade, registered MTR 164G. The tilt cab of these appliances may have made engine servicing easier but the technicians had to remember to half slip the escape first! The escape was by Merryweather and the appliance carried 200 gallons of water. Incidentally this vehicle carried no builder's plate of any description – the CFO would have no builder's 'advertising' on his vehicles. (*HCB-Angus*)

A very odd trio of appliances was ordered by Manchester Fire Brigade. While being standard PE appliances, the choice of Albion CH13EL as the chassis was anything but standard. Seen here yet to be fitted with its escape is s1719, registered JVU 592F, the first of the trio. (*HCB-Angus*)

1969 saw the Fijian authorities take delivery of a pair of Thornycroft Nubian CTs for the Nandi International Airport. Shown here posing in the New Forest is one of the pair – s1726 – painted, unusually, in white before shipping. These appliances carried 850 gallons of water, 200 of foam and a 200-lb dry-powder unit. (*HCB-Angus*)

Seen here at the Army Vehicle Research Centre at Chobham is Leicester City Fire Brigade's AEC WrT undertaking its tilt test. Carrying body s1740, the AEC was registered SBC 999G. Somewhat alarmingly, there do not seem to be any restraining straps fitted just in case it were to tip over! (*HCB-Angus*)

The forward-control Land Rover was infrequently used as a fire appliance, the normal control being favoured. However, the South African Department of Defence ordered five DP appliances on s1772. They were destined for munitions factories where their 2,000-lb dry-powder extinguishers were no doubt a comfort! (*HCB-Angus*)

The Ministry of Defense sought some light 4x4 appliances (L4P) and it fell to HCB-Angus to develop this appliance based on Land Rover's forward-control vehicle. The company had considerable difficulty in bringing the vehicle in within Land Rover's axle loading but got there in the end. Photographed is the first of the initial order of ten appliances, 1809, registered 22 FG 67, which served initially at RAEDE Woolwich. The appliance design was successful and further orders followed. (*HCB-Angus*)

Industrial plants continued to place orders for Transit-based L2Ps, in this case for the Central Electricity Generating Board's Rugely power station. S1833, registered PAA 998G, was based on the lighter single-wheel-axled version and carried a road engine-driven pump (by way of a PTO designed and built by HCB-Angus) fed from a 60-gallon tank. (*HCB-Angus*)

Showing its paces here is s1845, an ERF 84PFS 50-foot Simon Snorkel. This vehicle started out in life as a demonstrator for Simon Engineering as just an HP with a two-man cab in which guise it did the rounds. It was then purchased by Kent Fire Brigade who wished it to be a fully cabbed PHP. In order to achieve this the company had to completely replace the cab, install a pump (HCB-Angus's own) at the rear and build up a reworked body. Added to this there were some difficulties with the engineering in matching the hydraulic PTO and the pump PTO to the engine's characteristics but all was achieved eventually. (*HCB-Angus*)

Although it is now the late 1960s, the split-screen Bedford TK is going strong, as it was to do for more than twenty years more. Here is seen a single vehicle order (placed alongside an order for a number of WrTs) for a PE for the Devon Fire Brigade. Registered as OTT 309G, s1989 is seen here on station carrying both a 45-foot Merryweather escape and a 35-foot Bailey extension ladder. (*Gary Chapman*)

Lindsey County Fire Brigade specified this specially built Light Emergency Tender (LET) on a Land Rover S2 chassis. It was s2005 and was registered RFW 784H. (*HCB-Angus*)

A 60-foot Simon Platform built on a TK chassis for the City of Jordan. S2043 makes use of the standard cab for the driver and officer – the crew has a shelter to the rear – good job it's warm in those parts! Though the appliance had no main pump it did carry a light portable pump (LPP) in a side locker. (*HCB-Angus*)

In the early 1970s HCB-Angus offered a revision to the standard TK cab – it was purely cosmetic in the provision of a full-width, curved-glass windscreen as an alternative to the two-piece flat screen. It was sourced from the AEC parts bin as it was that fitted to the Matador cab of the day! The flat-screen version remained available for some time – until stocks of the screen glass were depleted. Shown here is one of an order for a dozen appliances placed in 1972 showing s2188 registered DYO 627J. (*Unknown*)

The Iraq military ordered fifteen Water Carriers (WC) based on the Ford D700 chassis cab. While HCB-Angus produced the pump engineering and bodywork, the provision of the elliptical tanks and their mounting was subcontracted out to Longwell Green in Bristol. (*HCB-Angus*)

Industrial appliances were a favourite within the works – no two were the same as they met specific needs. This one, s2241, registered 7764 NZ, was built for Monsanto Textiles on a Bedford TK and carried 100 gallons of water, 400 gallons of foam and a 300-lb dry-powder unit. The monitor, by Pyrene, is an impressive bit of kit! (*HCB-Angus*)

This short-wheelbase TK formed the underpinning of this large Dry Powder Unit (DPU). The steel sphere contains 2,000 lbs of dry powder and the nitrogen propellant is in the horizontal cylinder to the rear. The appliance was built on s2275 for the Egyptian Petroleum Company. (*HCB-Angus*)

The Kingdom of Bahrain, while being a small country, does not do things by halves when it comes to equipment. This ERF 84RS-chassised HP, s2323, carried an 85-foot Simon Engineering platform and also had the benefit of a full crew cab. Also carried were LPP suitable to feed the water tower contained within the Snorkel. Just what the purpose was of the oxygen cylinder strapped to the booms, is not known. (*HCB-Angus*)

Little is known of this pair of Land Rover forward-control DP appliances except that they were supplied to a customer in Syria. This one, s2330, identifies as not even being painted red so it may be assumed it was for an industrial user. (*HCB-Angus*)

The Ministry of Works ordered three of these appliances (though they were operated by the Navy) for escort duties when the military were moving atomic warheads around Great Britain. They were standard pumping appliances except they had no ladder racks fitted. Built on s2342, this one is registered 13 RN 31. (*HCB-Angus*)

Vauxhall Motors had to respond to the Ford Motor Company when they produced the Transit and this was the result. This Bedford CF was the HCB-Angus prototype on s2355 and after evaluation it went to Vauxhall Motors' proving ground as a Rapid Intervention Vehicle (RIV). It was never registered for road use. (*HCB-Angus*)

Rochdale Fire Brigade continued with its policy of painting the fronts of its vehicles white with this Emergency Salvage Tender (EST) built for them by HCB-Angus on s2421, on an ERF 84RF chassis. It carried a vast amount of kit, even an electric winch mounted to the front chassis member. The appliance was registered TDK 999K and passed to Greater Manchester Fire & Rescue Service in 1974 to see further service. (*HCB-Angus*)

About this time the whole of HCB-Angus had come under the control of the Dunlop Group, so when they needed an L4P for one of their factories it was natural to come to HCB-Angus for it. A standard appliance s2441 on a Land Rover S3 saw service at the Birmingham works but was never registered for road use. (*HCB-Angus*)

The Ministry of Technology commissioned HCB-Angus to produce a Truck Aircraft Rescue (TACR) appliance to replace the Forces' existing Land Rover-based machines and this was the result, produced against a very exacting specification. It carried a comprehensive set of rescue gear, 100 gallons of water and a Hathaway lightweight pump. The strange 'cabin' rear centre is for the last member of the crew who must have found it a very uncomfortable ride. This example is S2513, registered 28 AG 00, the prototype of an initial order for seventeen appliances though the company went on to produce nearly 100 for all branches of the armed services. (*HCB-Angus*)

Bootle Fire Brigade ordered an ET from the company on s5014, registered KEM 475K, on a Bedford TK chassis. It is a little unusual in as much as the bell is mounted low down on the extended front bumper, presumably for height restriction reasons. (*Unknown*)

Brecon & Radnorshire Joint Fire Brigade purchased this Bedford TK-based Hydraulic Platform (HP) fitted with Simon engineering 70-foot booms. It was built on s5027 and was registered FFO 606K. (*HCB-Angus*)

A new chassis for domestic appliance use, and one that was to become popular, was the Ford D series. This example for Surrey Fire Brigade on s5027, registered HPF 80K, was the first of an order for thirteen in 1971. The Ford had a tilt cab so the crew and driver compartment were separate apart from a hatch between the two for communication purposes. (*HCB-Angus*)

The Ministry of Defence specified a small domestic WrT for use on military bases and the company produced this appliance chassised on the light version of the Bedford TK – note the six stud wheels. They were fitted with only a 300-gallon tank, a 250-gpm Coventry Climax pump and a single hose reel mounted above the pump at the rear. The photograph is of the first of twenty-seven on this order, s5038 and registered 23 AJ 79. (*HCB-Angus*)

Leicester City Fire Brigade had a fondness for the AWEC 2TGM4R ordering a further example, s5042, registered CRY 999K. This appliance is seen here on the rally field having been preserved since coming out of service. (*HCB-Angus*)

An AEC 2TGM4R formed the basis for a special Emergency Tender (ET) for the City of Sheffield Fire Brigade, constructed on s1074, registered NEJ 578K. Note the extended front bumper, on which was mounted a winch, and the hydraulically powered crane fitted at the very rear of the chassis. (*HCB-Angus*)

A Leyland Beaver is the basis for this refinery vehicle, so chosen due to the antipathy shown to perceived American-based lorry builders by some Arab countries. The Iranian Oil Services ordered this large appliance that carried 400 gallons of foam compound and a 250-kg dry-powder installation. It was also fitted with transfer pumps so that the on-board foam tank could be refilled from storage tanks by the appliance itself. (*HCB-Angus*)

As mentioned earlier the constrictions of UK Construction and Use regulations and the JCDD specifications could be ignored by countries abroad. This water tender on a Bedford TK for Nigeria is just that – except that the tank size has been increased from 400 to 1,000 gallons. The company designated them T10 WrT and supplied many to African and other countries. (*HCB-Angus*)

Coventry Fire Brigade ordered a pair of standard Bedford WrTs on s5100 and it just so happened that HCB-Angus were developing a new scuttle for fitting to the Unipower chassis, which was itself under development. The company offered Coventry FB the chance to have the new scuttle fitted at no extra cost. This was accepted and here we see one of the pair YVC 355K having the new front fitted. (*HCB-Angus*)

This heavy-duty Bedford TK was ordered by South Eastern Fire Brigade (notice it has an extra locker each side) on s5105, registered XSG 847K. It carries somewhat more kit than a standard WrT (note the generator in the front locker), and as such was ordered with the Janspeed conversion kit for the engine to give the petrol engine a few more horsepower. (*HCB-Angus*)

At much the same time as the Ford D series of chassis appeared, Dodge produced the K850 series, very similar in style and specification. Glamorgan County Fire Brigade specified this chassis for the provision of six WrT appliances on s5128, this one being HTG 270L. (*Unknown*)

The Liberian military had previously ordered a pair of Land Rover appliances on s5005 but now added a third on s5143. It is seen here in the yard at the factory being kitted out. (*HCB-Angus*)

Lancashire County Fire Brigade preferred to go down the Ford route and ordered twelve in all on s5144 and s5145 using the D1616 chassis. A group of them are photographed here in the company's yard awaiting delivery. Note that some are wearing incorrect registration numbers – sorted out before delivery! (*HCB-Angus*)

51

The pair of appliances mentioned on page 28 – for the Chilean oil industry – were due for replacement and an order was duly placed with the company for this pair on s5167. On Ford D series chassis, the rather skeletal appliances carried 135 gallons of water, 442 of foam compound and a 300-lb dry-powder unit – together with a ladder perched atop the tank! The second axle conversion was by York. (*HCB-Angus*)

A Ford D600 was the basis for an ET built for Portsmouth City Fire Brigade on s5169, registered XBK 433L. The design was somewhat unusual with the rear step platform to gain access to the interior but also having a shelter for inclement weather! (*HCB-Angus*)

Portsmouth City Fire Brigade purchased a pair of Ford D1616 appliances on s5170, this one being TRV 912K. They were standard WrTs and were later absorbed into Hampshire control at the time of reorganisation. (*Unknown*)

Warwickshire ordered five WrTs on the Bedford TK chassis but opted for the Jaguar-engined option together with the 'upmarket' scuttle, this one being s5184, registered KNX 999L. Some 100 appliances were supplied with the Jaguar-engine conversion but it was a conversion plagued with overheating problems and not generally considered a success. (*HCB-Angus*)

The Bedford M, the 4x4 version of the TK, was as popular as its earlier brother, the R, and in this case is the basis for an ET for the Uganda Aerodrome Fire Service. It carried body s5238. (*HCB-Angus*)

This Land Rover ET was ordered by the City of Swansea Fire Brigade particularly with road traffic collisions in mind. On s5261 and registered KCY 261L, it was fitted with a Hydrovane compressor, hydraulically driven from the road engine to supply air for cutting gear and a winch. The Clark extending lighting mast could also be supplied from this but also had its own compressor for independent use. (*HCB-Angus*)

An odd pair of Airfield ETs was purchased by the Iranian Air Department on s5266. Utilising an Albion 4x4 chassis and fitted with the LAD (Leyland Albion Dodge) cab, it carried a generator and all the usual gear for penetrating crashed aircraft. It is not clear whether the vehicles were for military or civilian airfields. (*HCB-Angus*)

Seen here resting on a rally field, having been preserved, is Durham County Fire Brigade's ERF 84PF WrT RHN 999L, built in 1973 on s5274. (*Unknown*)

Cornwall County Fire Brigade ordered this Simon Snorkel-equipped Dodge K1050 on s5319, registration RCV 273M. The HP is an SS220 model having a reach of 77 feet, not the biggest of equipment but better suited to the narrow roads of Cornwall. (*Unknown*)

Hereford & Worcester Fire Brigade ordered a pair of Bedford TK WrTs on s5344, this being TFK 264M. A small extravagance – a chrome bumper – has been specified. (*HCB-Angus*)

This demonstrator was built on s5351 on the ubiquitous Ford Transit in twin-rear-wheel form. Having spent some time doing the rounds it was eventually sold to the Ford Motor Co. who used it solely on site, never registering it. (*HCB-Angus*)

The Nigerian Government, by way of the Crown Agency, ordered no less than ten of these Thornycroft Nubian CTs, eight on s5365 and a further two on s5366 for delivery in 1974. They were big machines carrying 1,400 gallons of water and 200 gallons of foam compound. One is seen here laying a foam carpet for a crash-landing plane. (*HCB-Angus*)

The Rover Company ordered this Land Rover-based appliance for its own works (they could hardly specify another chassis!). Registered RXC 646M on s5372, it carried 90 gallons of water and had a PTO-driven Coventry Climax pump. (*HCB-Angus*)

In the search for a faster vehicle to use as an alternative to the Land Rover the company was offered the Dodge Powerwagon as a basis for fast road, and capable 4x4 off-road, vehicles. To start off with, the company opted for the lighter of the two specifications (single rear wheels on the rear axle), the W300 option. On this they constructed a Rapid Intervention Vehicle (RIV) as a demonstrator. Seeking some publicity, they christened the resultant vehicle the 'Firestreak' and Corgi produced a large-scale model with some innovative features. The photograph is of the prototype vehicle on s5376, and after some time doing the demonstration rounds it was refurbished as s5571 and went to the Cayman Islands to serve on their airport. (*HCB-Angus*)

The Emirate of Oman purchased a number of Thornycroft Nubian Major-chassised CTs. This is one of a pair ordered on s5378 that saw service at Seeb International Airport. It, and its companion, carried 1,400 gallons of water and 200 gallons of foam compound. (*HCB-Angus*)

BP Norway ordered a pair of FoTs on s5399 for their refinery operations. They were built on the heaviest of the Dodge K series, the KT900, with a third axle added by York. They had a single tank constructed to carry 900 gallons of foam compound, relying on the site's hydrant supply for water with which to generate foam using the Coventry Climax pump. (*HCB-Angus*)

British Steel's works at Trostre purchased this Land Rover-based appliance on s5411. It was registered GEP 192N. Note the side-mounted pump control and deliveries, the pump being mounted amidships, leaving the rear door clear. (*HCB-Angus*)

Unipower introduced the Invader chassis as a firefighting vehicle chassis in 1972 and the company developed this CT (recognise the scuttle?). The Malaysian authorities ordered ten of them on s5411 for distribution to the country's airports. They carried 1,000 gallons of water and 100 gallons of foam compound. The first is seen here undergoing off-road trials at FVRE Chobham. (*HCB-Angus*)

MFA 472P was one of seven appliances purchased by Staffordshire Fire Brigade in 1974 on s5454 on Ford D114 chassis. Though the ladder is missing from the appliance in the photograph, the machine should be carrying a 45-foot alloy ladder, which had, over the years, replaced the 35-foot wooden-trussed ladder. In this form, the official terminology was Water Tender Ladder (WrT/L). (*Unknown*)

Dodge G11 chassis were the basis for a dozen appliances purchased by Devon Fire Brigade on s5507. A rather conservative design, the appliances sported slam lids for the lockers and retained the trussed ladder as top gear. This example, seen just prior to delivery, was registered LTT 196P. (*Gary Chapman*)

Thornycroft Super Majors must have taken up a lot of room in the works during production. This one was for the Emirate of Dubai on s5517 and carried 1,500 gallons of water and 200 of foam compound. (*HCB-Angus*)

Refinery vehicles continued to be steadily produced by the company. This one, for Philips Petroleum, s5527 registered MAJ 161P, carried 850 gallons of water and 170 of foam compound. (*HCB-Angus*)

The Sultanate of Oman purchased a pair of these interesting-looking RIVs based on the Dodge W300 for use on the country's airfields. Built on s5532 the pair carried a 500-lb dry-powder unit and the crew travelled in the open-sided compartment to the rear of the vehicle. (*HCB-Angus*)

Cambridgeshire Fire & Rescue Service bought a number of Dodge-based WrLs over the years, this being the 1975 purchase, s5604, for four appliances. This is LVE 773P seen on service in Cambridge. (*HCB-Angus*)

Swaziland Fire & Emergency Services favoured chrome yellow for their appliances and this one, s5626, was true to the mould. Obtained by way of the Crown Agents it was delivered late in 1975 as a WrT though notice that all the ladders are of alloy – a precaution given the environment. (*HCB-Angus*)

Guyana Fire Service took delivery of six of these Bedford WrTs (s5649) based on the new body style that was being devised for the Crew Safety Vehicle. These were not CSVs but utilised the same skinning panels over a conventional all-metal frame – they just looked like CSVs! Underneath they were standard petrol-engined WrTs. (*HCB-Angus*)

The TACR1, featured earlier, saw several repeat orders over the years. The Ministry ordered a pair in this case, s5651, now based on the Land Rover Series Three. This one, registered 91 RN 48, as the other Navy examples, was painted Post Office Red. (*HCB-Angus*)

The Egyptian authorities ordered a pair of Land Rover L4Ps on s5706. They were of the standard pattern, having a 60-gallon water tank and a PTO-driven Coventry Climax pump. Their eventual destination is not known. (*HCB-Angus*)

The Crew Safety Vehicle, the first fire engine specifically designed to safeguard the crew by having considerable cab crash resistance, had been introduced and the Fire Service Training College, Moreton-in-Marsh, was provided with one by the Home Office. Built on s5727 and registered OYH 414R, the vehicle was to spend some years at the college before passing to Merseyside Fire Brigade for driver-training purposes. (*HCB-Angus*)

When times were quiet the company would contract itself to build vehicles and hold them in stock against future purchases. S5732 is one such order, for three RIV vehicles on the Dodge W400. The one photographed here was shortly afterwards sold to the Emirate of Dubai on s5751. The W400 was a far more capable machine than the W300 having double rear wheels and a generally stronger capability. (*HCB-Angus*)

The Ministry of Defence placed, rather strangely, an order for a single Bedford WrT on s5766, the more usual order being for several at a time. Registered 31 AG 44, the vehicle was painted matt green. (*HCB-Angus*)

This massive refinery vehicle was built for Occidental Oil Company based in Libya on s5780, a Bedford TM 6x4 chassis. Capable of dealing with the largest refinery fire it carried no less than 600 gallons of water, a similar amount of foam compound and a 750-lb dry-powder installation. Delivery was by way of no less than eight hand lines as well as the monitor. (*HCB-Angus*)

Seen here on station on the Isle of Wight is s5877, registered YDL 999T, one of several CSVs purchased by the Isle of Wight Fire Brigade. HCB-Angus had decided on the white paint specification for the demonstrator vehicles and it was taken up by many brigades who purchased them. The Isle of Wight appliances did eventually become red, however. (*HCB-Angus*)

Buckinghamshire Fire Brigade ordered a trio of Dodge G13-chassised appliances late in 1978 on s5875. Standard WrL in configuration, the G13 series were generally considered better vehicles than the K series they had replaced. One of the three, registered ENM 626T, is seen here in a later life with Amersham International PLC, to whom it was loaned by the brigade. (*HCB-Angus*)

The company took a leap of faith in developing a new prototype CT on the newly introduced Thornycroft Nubian Major Mk2 (though, due to company mergers it emerged as a Scammell product). A totally new chassis concept for the company as the chassis was a rear-engined 6x6 arrangement. The body design was advanced in concept for its day (1980) and was well received. The appliance was sold to Air Rianta and served all its life at Cork International Airport were it ran registered as 960 DZB. It carried 1,000 gallons of water and 200 of foam compound and had an array of mounted and handheld branches for foam delivery. (*HCB-Angus*)

This Bedford TK-based WrFoT was originally ordered by a customer on s5798 but was cancelled part way through the build. It was, however, sold on as s5904 to the Emirate of Dubai for service at their dry-dock complex. It carried 900 gallons of water and 75 of foam compound. Just how the firefighters were supposed to reach those hose reels is anyone's guess! (*HCB-Angus*)

Much smaller in stature than the Scammell was this Control Unit (CU) built on s5946 for Shropshire Fire Service. The chassis used was Ford's A series and was to feature in several more appliances over the years. (*HCB-Angus*)

67

The design of Land Rover appliance, though diverse in specification, had not changed greatly; slam lockers for instance were the norm. The company, on s5938, devised a prototype with totally different locker arrangements, substituting a gas-sprung, top-hinged bin to replace the hinged locker doors. The concept worked well apart from attraction the nickname 'fish fryer lockers' due to a certain resemblance! This prototype was joined by some fourteen more on s5985 to fill an order for the Iranian Oil Authority. Technically the specification had not changed, but the body had become for more modern looking. (*HCB-Angus*)

County of Avon Fire Brigade purchased four Dodge G1313-based appliances on s6000 as standard WrL. Notice that the bell has now gone as the audible warning of approach and has been replaced by electronic yelp warnings – hence the roof-mounted tannoy. (*HCB-Angus*)

British Airways operated this CSV appliance at Heathrow Airport. It was the only one so configured, being a cross between a crash tender and a domestic appliance. It was built on s6024 and carried 400 gallons of premixed foam/water in its tank to supply the monitor. (*HCB-Angus*)

This three-quarter rear view of the Dodge W400 RIV shows how the equipment is stowed to advantage. This particular example, s6001, went to serve the Trinidad and Tobago Airport Authority. (*HCB-Angus*)

The People's Republic of China ordered five standard L4P appliances on Land Rover chassis on s6035. The photo shows three of them protected ready for the sea crossing to China. Shipping by sea required considerable packing in all cases – in part for protection and in part as anti-theft precautions. In this case the appliances were travelling as deck cargo, so protection from the elements was important. (*HCB-Angus*)

Occasionally customers required chassis that were the norm in the country of operation but not in the UK, and this required importation of a suitable chassis. This was the case in the requirement for a pair of Mercedes-bonneted vehicles for Iran Oil Services. The Mercedes L1513 WrTs built on s6046 were a case in point; the production of the vehicles took a considerable time due entirely to the negotiations required in the importation and subsequent exportation of the completed product. (*HCB-Angus*)

It was unusual to convert a standard Bedford TK rather than start off with the M type but this is what was done here for North Yorkshire Fire Service in 1980. The body was standard WrT on the civilian chassis and body, but given a 4x4 capability. It was s6050 and registered KVN 296W. (*HCB-Angus*)

Lucas Industries purchased this standard L4P on s6053, registered GOK 251W. The addition of a Francis Searchlight, and the larger version at that, did nothing for the lines of the vehicle! (*HCB-Angus*)

Pertamina, the Malaysian state-owned oil and gas-production company, ordered a trio of WrFoTs constructed on the uprated and extended Bedford TK chassis. Built on s6080 the trio carried 750 gallons of water and 75 of foam compound. Notice that the cab is standard Bedford; the peaked top was, in fact, built over the top of the original. (*HCB-Angus*)

Tipperary County Council Fire Service ordered a pair of HCB-Angus new High Strength Cab versions of the evergreen Bedford TK. The new scuttle, not produced in house for the first time, fronted a cab reinforced with steel tubing to give greatly improved crash resistance without going to the super levels of the CSV. The one, photographed on leaving the factory for delivery, was registered 998 BFI. (*HCB-Angus*)

Surrey Fire Brigade ordered five WrTs based on the Shelvoke & Drewry chassis, more usually associated with refuse lorries and the like. The company manufactured a tilt-cab arrangement, which they had first developed for the Dodge appliances, whereby the complete cab, crew section included, tilted as one. This made for unparalleled access to the engine but also for a very heavy structure that was supported on gas struts. The order was on s6155 and the first, registered SPM 112X, is photographed here prior to delivery. (*HCB-Angus*)

HCB-Angus had been a leader in the production of the TACR1 appliance for the Forces but was not so with its successor, the 6x4 Range Rover-based TACR2, this falling to Gloster Saro. They did, however, secure an order for eighteen in the second round of tendering. The development vehicle was s6159, registered 94 AM 37. Shown is one of the bulk of the order, registered 51 AG 48, on s6163. (*HCB-Angus*)

Seen here from an unusual viewpoint is the High Strength Cab Bedford TK that was produced for the United Kingdom Atomic Energy Authority. Built on s6160, registered WUD 267X, it carried water, foam compound and, unusually, BCF extinguishant. (*HCB-Angus*)

The Malaysian Air Ministry ordered six of the these Scammell Super Nubian appliances (s6165) on a very tight delivery schedule – so much so that much of the design work for the body was done on the shop floor during construction! They carried 1,200 gallons of water and 120 of foam compound, together with roof-mounted monitor, hand lines and underbody drenching nozzles. The paint finish was in Sunshine Yellow. (*HCB-Angus*)

The parking up of completed vehicles awaiting delivery was always a problem for the company – here we see no less than eight Bedford HSC WrTs awaiting delivery or collection. The first in line is s6170 for Cork County Fire Service, ordered on s6170 and registered 438 OZB. (*HCB-Angus*)

Final Years

By the 1980s, things were a little different; the economic climate had taken a change much for the worse and sales were down, chassis demands were calling for heavier and more powerful offerings, safety concerns called for redesigns and foreign customers were requiring chassis that were available in the country of operation. Bedford, Dodge and Ford continued to provide the bulk of the chassis, suitably uprated by the provision of bigger engines (by now universally diesel). Bedford had 'caught up' with the TL, a tilt-cab version of the TK, though the company did not make a tilting-cabbed version as it would have been costly to develop – they just fixed the cab down!

The end of the decade saw Vauxhall Motors cease production of commercial vehicles and the general decline of commercial-vehicle production by UK builders so allowing the continental onslaught. Volvo, Scania and Mercedes were to feature widely during the last decade of the company's life in the supply of local authority appliances. The Military Bedford chassis, still being available, enabled the company to continue supplying to those markets throughout this period.

ICI Dupont ordered a Foam Tender (FoT) on a high-strength-cab Bedford. As can be seen from the photo, the monitor is operated from a position above the pump and there are no less than six deliveries for hand lines. Built on s6175 the appliance does not appear to have been registered. [*HCB-Angus*]

The Isle of Wight Fire Brigade was one of the first to take delivery of Bedford's new TL-chassised vehicles. Bedford had produced this as an urgent advancement on the TK, as a tilt cab was a necessity to stay in the market place. However, in HCB-Angus's hands it remained as a fixed cab as the technical difficulties were deemed to be not worth pursuing. VDL 190Y, s6180, was a single vehicle order and, as can be seen, the Isle of Wight still retained its white identity at this time. (HCB-Angus)

The Emirate of Oman ordered a pair of these Mercedes-based CTs for Oman International Airport on s6285 while they had, at the same time, ordered, on the same model chassis, a pair of WrTs (s6284) and a pair of FoTs (s6286). Having a commonality of chassis must have saved cost and time for all concerned! (HCB-Angus)

Competition for the Ford A-series chassis came from Dodge in the shape of the S66 series, on which chassis Leicestershire Fire & Rescue Service ordered a pair of Rescue Tenders (RT) on s6200. The pair carried the usual rescue equipment seen on such vehicles, and had a 2.5-kW generator by Powermite to power the Clark extending lighting mast and other equipment. (*HCB-Angus*)

Reynolds Broughton was a small operation building specialist chassis, and it is on a pair of their RB44 chassis that HCB-Angus built Medium Crash Tenders (MCT) for Exeter Airport on s6203. They carried 220 gallons of water and 70 of foam compound and had a monitor remotely controlled from within the cab. (*HCB-Angus*)

The Indonesian Government purchased a pair of Foam Carriers (FoC), based on Bedford 6x4 TM chassis, the order being on s6208. They had no direct firefighting capability, not having a pumping system. The tank was of 1,665-gallon capacity and the vehicle did have Albany gear pumps for the filling of and transferring of compound to and from the tank. (*HCB-Angus*)

This very unusual vehicle was not for firefighting but potentially for crowd control in the UK. Ordered by Her Majesty's Government on s6213, it was to be an evaluation vehicle and as such was built to a comprehensive specification. Underneath that body is a 6x4 Bedford TM carrying a 2,000-gallon water tank with a Coventry Climax pump (driven from a separate Ford engine). Dye could be added to the water for later identification of personnel. The crew are in an air-conditioned (positive pressure) cab, can control the monitors remotely and have cameras that record what the water is pointing at! The vehicle was evaluated at the Police Training College at Hendon but was never brought into service. (*HCB-Angus*)

Warwickshire Fire & Rescue Service ordered this 91-foot Simon Hydraulic Platform chassised on a Shelvoke and Drewry 240 chassis. It was registered DVC 274Y and was built on s6219.

Though the Bedford TL chassis had by this time been introduced, there were still many TK chassis to be had, presumably at a discount! Oxfordshire Fire Brigade ordered eight appliances in 1983, four on s6225 and four on s6226. Shown here is one from the first batch, registered B646 VUD. Oxfordshire FB had, with this batch, moved from jackknife crew doors to the slam type. This appliance, together with many of its brothers, went to Malta to serve with the Civil Protection, Malta's Fire Service. (*HCB-Angus*)

The Indonesian authorities ordered this unusual Land Rover appliance, unusual inasmuch as it not only had a Coventry Climax front-mounted pump but also a hose reel pump driven directly off the gearbox, fed from a 60-gallon tank that was not plumbed to the main pump. It was built on s6229. (*HCB-Angus*)

This Mercedes 1625-based appliance was supplied on s6232 to Getty Oil in Kuwait. It was a Foam Dry Powder (FoDP) unit carrying 750 kg of dry powder and 350 gallons of foam compound. (*HCB-Angus*)

Another Land Rover for foreign parts, s6240 was built for the Emirate of Oman. Note the large number of extinguishers carried on the extended front bumper – in such a hot country this can have done nothing for engine cooling! (*HCB-Angus*)

Supplied for Pertamina in Indonesia was this ET, s6263, built on the light Bedford TK chassis. It had a generator mounted in the nearside locker driven by a jack shaft from the gearbox PTO. (*HCB-Angus*)

A rather handsome pair of Bedford M appliances – they quite suit the white wheels, bumpers and cab roofs, built for Shell Oil for their Malaysian operations on s6268. They carried 400 gallons of water and a 250-lb dry-powder installation. (*HCB-Angus*)

The Bedford TK-based appliances keep on coming! Northamptonshire Fire Brigade ordered a pair of High Strength Cabbed WrTs on s6270, this one being registered A999 XBD for 1984. (*HCB-Angus*)

The Emirate of Abu Dhabi (the largest of the emirates that make up the United Arab Emirates) ordered thirty of these vehicles. While strictly not firefighting vehicles, they do carry an engine-driven Coventry Climax fire pump driven by the road engine – which defines them as fire appliances! They were constructed as Water Carriers (WC) to alleviate the distribution shortages that the country was experiencing. This one, s6291, was the prototype, built on a Bedford KM 6x6 with a tank capacity of 3,000 gallons followed by the main order on s6292 for a further twenty-nine. (*HCB-Angus*)

The Malaysian authorities ordered twenty-two of these little appliances on the lightweight TL chassis on s6303. They carried 100 gallons of water and a 200-gpm Coventry Climax pump. The deadline for delivery for these appliances was so tight that HCB-Angus had to subcontract some of the body building to Carmichael Ltd with whom they usually competed! (*HCB-Angus*)

This Dodge W400 RIV, s6313, was purchased by Aero Associates, Anglesey, for use on its airport on the island. Unregistered while in service, it was given the registration number Q616 NTR later in life. (*HCB-Angus*)

The Bahraini authorities ordered a single Dennis SS-chassised WrT in 1986 on s6331, seen here in the rain near the factory – not what it would be used to, once delivered! The appliance was specified with twin Clarke masts for illumination, seen here extended to full height. (*HCB-Angus*)

Oxfordshire Fire Brigade maintained its allegiance to Bedford with an order for three WrTs on the TL chassis. Seen here, on s6346, the three appliances D810, D811, D812 OBW are waiting for the collection drivers to arrive. (*HCB-Angus*)

In 1986 the British Virgin Isles Fire & Rescue Service ordered just about an entire fire brigade. Among them was a pair of Land Rover 110 appliances, s6351, each carrying 75 gallons of water, a Coventry Climax pump and a ladder by Gravity. This one was registered GVO 204. An odd request was for the appliances to be equipped with two, stowed, empty five-gallon containers in which foam compound could be carried. (*HCB-Angus*)

As a further part of the replenishment of the BVI equipment, a pair a Bedford CF pick-up trucks were modified to work as small water carriers by the fitting (together with suitable valving) of 200-gallon-capacity flexible pillow tanks. This example was registered GVO 210. (*HCB-Angus*)

West Yorkshire Fire Service received a trio of ETs during the year. They were supposed to be chassised on the Bedford TL 570 but, as they could not deliver these lightweights, Bedford supplied TL 750 chassis at no additional cost – to West Yorkshire's advantage! Unlike the majority of HCB-Angus work they did not receive coach-built cabs, but basic commercial body building standards were used for the box body. (*HCB-Angus*)

The Dodge Powerwagons having become no longer available in the UK, the company moved to the GMC 30 as a basis for small rapid-intervention vehicles. This Rescue Unit for Bedfordshire Fire service, s6367, registered E933 YBH, was the first of a handful of these chassis to be converted, in this case to a Rescue Tender for motorway use in particular. (*HCB-Angus*)

Trintoc (Trinidad Oil Company) ordered a standard Land Rover S3 appliance on s6371 – standard, that is, apart from the white stripe along both sides of the body, this to distinguish it from the local authority appliances. (*HCB-Angus*)

The Bedford chassis in 4x2 form having become unavailable, due to the shock decision by Vauxhall Motors to cease manufacture, meant a new chassis had to be found, though in fact the company had already been working with the Volvo FL614. West Yorkshire Fire Service ordered an initial group of seven WrT appliances built on this chassis on s6382, this particular appliance being registered E182 DVH. The Volvo was to become the backbone of domestic WrT/L production until production ceased some seven years later. (*HCB-Angus*)

The 4x4 Bedford M was still available. A complex bit of manoeuvring saw AWD buy the rights to build TL-styled machines carrying the AWD logo, but M types still continued as Bedfords. Eventually AWD also ceased to exist but then Marshalls of Cambridge retained the right to manufacture the M type, mostly for military purposes. Here we have an M type for the Saudi European Petroleum Company basking in the sunlight late one afternoon. Built on s6388 as an FoT, it carried 500 gallons of foam compound. (*HCB-Angus*)

Oxfordshire Fire Service maintained their allegiance to HCB-Angus and when the Bedfords became unavailable they moved across to Volvo. This is one of the four ordered on s6400 as WrL, registered E572 AJO. (*HCB-Angus*)

The company returned to the concept of the Lo Cost vehicle referred to earlier in completing an order for the MoD for nine WrTs utilising the Bedford TL chassis, now becoming scarce. A later order for more of these vehicles required a change of chassis, the nine were completed on s6409, this unit being registered 48 KG 71. (*HCB-Angus*)

Glaxo Pharmaceuticals PLC ordered this L4P on a Transit chassis/cowl as an L4P carrying 90 gallons of water. As before, a drive line PTO brought the drive up into the cargo compartment to drive the Coventry Climax pump directly. Built on s6416, registered F85 WRV. Notice how the top-hinged door has been dispensed with entirely. (*HCB-Angus*)

Bedfordshire Fire & Rescue Service were strong customers of HCB-Angus, regularly placing orders with the company. Here we have one of the standard WrTs on Volvo FL614 chassis ordered on s6419 as an order for three appliances. (*HCB-Angus*)

A further purchase by Glaxo Pharmaceuticals PLC was for a larger Pump (P). Based on the Dodge S66, and built as s6420, registered F818 XJT, 150 gallons of water were carried to feed the main pump. (*HCB-Angus*)

An usual choice of chassis was this Ford Cargo for an FoT for Associated Octel Ltd. Built on s6428, it carried 500 gallons of foam compound forward of the monitor turret. It was registered G679 CFX. (*HCB-Angus*)

The Rover Company purchased a couple of interesting 6x6 versions of the Land Rover Defender, of which this was the first, for their Land Rover plant. No fixed pump was installed but a Light Portable pump was carried together with a foam installation, so one assumes the factory water main would provide the water. Built on s6438, it was registered G600 WAC. (*HCB-Angus*)

The Dodge G1313s were now wearing Renault badges, but the appliance remained the same underneath, this being one of three ordered late in 1989 by Cornwall Fire Service. This is the last of the three on s6443, registered G745 CAF. (*HCB-Angus*)

The Nigerian authorities ordered three FoTs in 1990 on s6452 for their Oil Industries to be constructed on the military Bedford M chassis. The three are seen here packed up and ready to be shipped as deck cargo. They were built on s6452. (*HCB-Angus*)

The Kingdom of Bahrain ordered four of these Dennis SS appliances for their city authorities on s6453. They were standard water tenders, only uprated with larger engine radiators to assist in coping with the conditions to be found in the kingdom. (*HCB-Angus*)

Das Island is a tiny island off the coast of, and part of, the Emirate of Abu Dhabi. The island is given over solely to the production of petroleum products. Adma Opco operated this Mercedes 1922 WrFoT on s6457. It carried 400 gallons each of water and foam compound. (*HCB-Angus*)

Bedfordshire Fire & Rescue Service contacted HCB-Angus to build this unique L4P on s6467, consulting with the company right through the design and manufacturing process. Technically it was not special having a Coventry Climax pump driven from the road engine drawing water from an on-board tank. The uniqueness came from the locker design of s6467, registered H906 HUR, as it used full-length roller shutters each side. (*HCB-Angus*)

Another brigade unable to source Dennis-bodied appliances at this time was Northamptonshire Fire Service, who had a pair of chassis bodied by the company. Built on s6472, this one is registered H582 CNH. (*HCB-Angus*)

Another odd chassis imported for the purpose was this 1,000-gallon WrT for the Ugandan authorities. It was built on a bonneted Mercedes chassis on s6473. (*HCB-Angus*)

Some brigades wanted what they perceived to be a tougher chassis than the Volvo, and South Glamorgan County Fire Service picked the Scania 93H as the basis for a pair of Rescue Pumps (RP), so called as they carried more rescue gear in addition to the normal WrT equipment. Note the continental-style wheel rims fitted to just this pair of appliances. (*HCB-Angus*)

The Renault Dodge Midliner seemed to offer a halfway point between the somewhat light Volvo and the heavy Scania, and it was specified for Greater Manchester Fire & Rescue Service for seven WrLs. The company spent some time developing the appliance and the result was quite pleasing to the eye. They were built on s6510 and this one was photographed fresh from the paint shop and ready for kitting out. (*HCB-Angus*)

West Glamorgan County Fire Service was another authority to embrace the pod system for minority application equipment. This pod contained 500 gallons of foam plus the equipment to go with it. The prime mover was a Scania G93M – not fitted out by HCB-Angus. The pod was built on s6519. (*HCB-Angus*)

Volvo FS7 was built for Dorset Fire & Rescue Service as a Rescue Pump (RP). Note the winch mounted on the forward ends of the chassis. Apart from the rescue equipment, the appliance carried a complement of usual firefighting equipment. (*HCB-Angus*)

Cornwall Fire & Rescue Service decided on a pair of 4x4 Mercedes 112AF pumps to serve in the central, rather rural, areas where a 4x4 might well be of advantage. The company built them on s6526, the one photographed being L214 VRL. A further pair was ordered almost immediately on s6527. (*HCB-Angus*)

Hampshire Fire & Rescue Service had always had a good working relationship with the company – their workshops being literally just down the road. The last order to be placed with the company was for four Volvo FL614 WrLs. The four were built on s6531 and this one was an exception inasmuch as it did not share the same specification as the other three. Registered L84 RTP, it was fitted with a 1000-gpm pump rather than the usual 500-gpm version. (*HCB-Angus*)

As HCB-Angus was about to come to the end of its production life it received an order from Tyne and Wear Fire & Rescue Service and thus built its last 'special', an ET for that brigade. Based on the Volvo FL614, it was a large appliance fitted with all manner of kit. During service it saw several changes in colour scheme and was finally withdrawn from service late in 2012 after nearly 20 years' service! (*HCB-Angus*)

Facts and Figures

Total number of vehicles produced   Approx. 6,500 units
Most prolific chassis provider   Bedford – 2,999 units of all types
Most prolific chassis   Bedford TK series – 1,770 units
Least prolific chassis provider   Reynolds Boughton – 3 units
Least prolific chassis   Mercedes Unimog – 1 unit

The Database

It is not possible to include the database of all the appliances produced by HCB-Angus due to its size. If the reader would like to obtain a copy containing the full database on a CD-ROM then he should contact the author on this email address for further information: aidanfisher@yahoo.com Enquiries will be dealt with promptly.

FIRE APPLIANCE

ON DODGE KEW TYPE CHASSIS

HAMPSHIRE CAR BODIES LTD.

TOTTON · HANTS · ENGLAND

Telephone: TOTTON 3141